MW00914651

Monet

2000

DELUXE ENGAGEMENT BOOK

National Gallery of Art, Washington

Catalog No. 200006

Published by Pomegranate Communications, Inc., Box 6099, Rohnert Park, California 94927

© 1999 Board of Trustees, National Gallery of Art, Washington

All works of art included in this calendar are from the collections of the
National Gallery of Art, Washington

❧

Available in Canada from Firefly Books Ltd.,

3680 Victoria Park Avenue, Willowdale, Ontario M2H 3K1

Available in the U.K. and mainland Europe from Pomegranate Europe Ltd.,

Fullbridge House, Fullbridge, Maldon, Essex CM9 4LE, England

Available in Australia from Boobook Publications Pty. Ltd.,

P.O. Box 163 or Freepost 1, Tea Gardens 2324

Available in New Zealand from Randy Horwood Ltd.,

P.O. Box 32-077, Devonport, Auckland

Available in Asia (including the Middle East), Africa, and Latin America from

Pomegranate International Sales, 113 Babcombe Drive,

Thornhill, Ontario L3T 1M9, Canada

❧

Pomegranate also publishes for 2000 the wall calendars *Claude Monet, The Impressionist Woman,* and *Renoir.*
Full-color catalogs of our calendars, notecards, boxed notes, notecard folios, postcards,
books of postcards, address books, books of days, posters, art magnets, Knowledge Cards™,
bookmarks, journals, and books are available at a nominal fee.
For more information on obtaining catalogs and ordering, please contact:

Pomegranate Communications, Inc.

Box 6099, Rohnert Park, California 94927

800 227 1428

www.pomegranate.com

Cover and graphic element:

The Artist's Garden in Argenteuil (A Corner of the Garden with Dahlias) (detail), 1873

Designed by Harrah Argentine

PRINTED IN KOREA

Moon phases and American, Canadian, and UK holidays are noted.
All astronomical data supplied in this calendar are expressed in Greenwich Mean Time (GMT)

$\mathcal{C}$LAUDE MONET (1840–1926) ranks among the greatest painters in the history of art. He was the most influential of the impressionists, a group of painters who strove to capture the endless variations of light and atmosphere found in nature. His career spanned a revolution that was predicated on an intensification of realism and going beyond that eventually led the way to abstraction.

Monet was born in Paris, France, and spent his youth in the coastal town of Le Havre, where he met his first teacher, the landscape painter Eugène Boudin (1824–1898). Boudin was an advocate of plein air painting, in which the artist paints outdoors, directly from nature, and he introduced Monet to this technique. Monet's later coastscape paintings reflect his boyhood exposure to Le Havre's maritime atmosphere.

Monet moved to Paris in 1862. Three years later, two of his paintings were highly praised at the prestigious Salon of the French Academy of Painting and Sculpture, but the jury later rejected his monumental canvas *Women in the Garden* (1866), deeming its subject "banal" and the technique unacceptable. Nevertheless, Monet's impressionist technique and vision evolved rapidly and had matured by 1872, when he moved to Argenteuil with his wife and frequent model, Camille Doncieux, and their son, Jean. His famous work *Impression, Sunrise,* which gave the impressionist movement its name, was painted that year. By the spring of 1873, Monet and his painter colleagues, including Degas, Morisot, Pissarro, Renoir, and Sisley, had begun to organize an artists' cooperative in order to escape the conservatism of the Salon. The group's first exhibition opened in Paris in April 1874, and the impressionists went on to present seven more exhibitions.

In 1883, four years after the death of Camille, Monet moved to a house in Giverny with Jean and Michel, his and Camille's second son. In 1892 he married Alice Hoschedé, the widow of his early patron, Ernest Hoschedé. Already a successful painter, Monet turned for his subject matter to the poppy fields, poplars, bridges, and wheatstacks of the surrounding countryside. He recorded in paint the changing light and atmospheric conditions to create distinctly different impressions of the same views.

Monet bought the house in Giverny in 1890 and established extensive gardens on the property, including a water garden filled with waterlilies and spanned by a Japanese footbridge. The waterlilies and bridge became the subjects of a series of paintings on which Monet worked from 1899 until his death, in 1926. In these works he transcended the earlier concerns of impressionism and achieved a style and structure that presaged the radical insights of modern art. At age eighty-six and nearly blind, Monet devoted himself to his spectacular water lilies murals, his final concern. After his death they were installed at the Orangerie in Paris, a gift from the artist to the French state. ❧

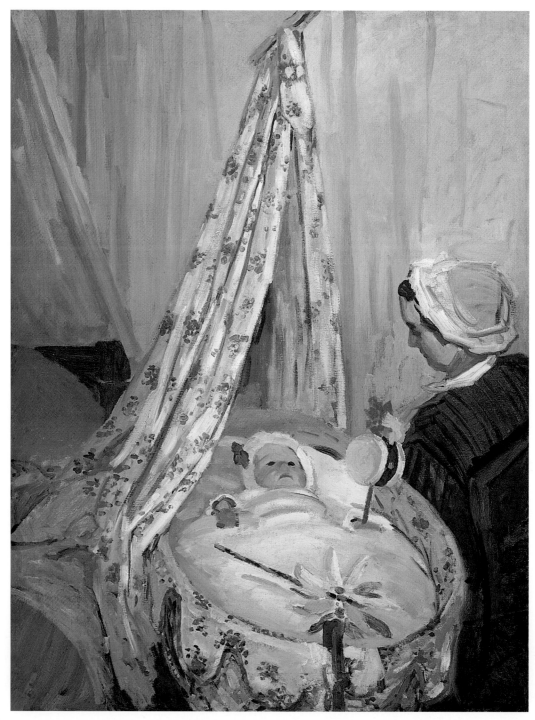

THE CRADLE—CAMILLE WITH THE ARTIST'S SON JEAN, *1867*

Oil on canvas, 116.2 x 88.8 cm
Collection of Mr. and Mrs. Paul Mellon
1983.1.25

DECEMBER ❧ JANUARY

27

MONDAY

362

28

TUESDAY

363

29

LAST QUARTER MOON

WEDNESDAY

364

30

THURSDAY

365

31

FRIDAY

NEW YEAR'S DAY

1

1

SATURDAY

2

2

SUNDAY

JANUARY	S	M	T	W	T	F	S
							1
	2	3	4	5	6	7	8
	9	10	11	12	13	14	15
	16	17	18	19	20	21	22
	23	24	25	26	27	28	29
	30	31					

NOTES

JANUARY

3	BANK HOLIDAY (UK)

3
MONDAY

4	BANK HOLIDAY (SCOTLAND ONLY)

4
TUESDAY

5

5
WEDNESDAY

6	

6
THURSDAY

NEW MOON

7

7
FRIDAY

8

8
SATURDAY

9

9
SUNDAY

NOTES

JANUARY

10

10
MONDAY

11

11
TUESDAY

12

12
WEDNESDAY

13

13
THURSDAY

14

14

FIRST QUARTER MOON

MARTIN LUTHER KING JR.'S BIRTHDAY

FRIDAY

15

15
SATURDAY

16

16
SUNDAY

JANUARY

S	M	T	W	T	F	S
					1	2
3	4	5	6	7	8	9
10	11	12	13	14	15	16
17	18	19	20	21	22	23
24	25	26	27	28	29	30
31						

NOTES

SAINTE-ADRESSE, *1867*

Oil on canvas, 57 x 80 cm
Gift (Partial and Promised) in Honor of the 50th Anniversary of the National Gallery of Art
1990.59.1

JANUARY

MARTIN LUTHER KING JR. DAY   *17*

17
MONDAY

18

18
TUESDAY

19

19
WEDNESDAY

20

20
THURSDAY

21

21
FRIDAY

FULL MOON

22

22
SATURDAY

23

23
SUNDAY

JANUARY

S	M	T	W	T	F	S
						1
2	3	4	5	6	7	8
9	10	11	12	13	14	15
16	17	18	19	20	21	22
23	24	25	26	27	28	29
30	31					

NOTES

JANUARY

24

24
MONDAY

25

25
TUESDAY

26

26
WEDNESDAY

27

27
THURSDAY

28

28
FRIDAY   LAST QUARTER MOON

29

29
SATURDAY

30

30
SUNDAY

NOTES

31

31

MONDAY

32

1

TUESDAY

33

2

WEDNESDAY

34

3

THURSDAY

35

4

FRIDAY

36

5

SATURDAY

NEW MOON

37

6

SUNDAY

FEBRUARY	S	M	T	W	T	F	S
			1	2	3	4	5
	6	7	8	9	10	11	12
	13	14	15	16	17	18	19
	20	21	22	23	24	25	26
	27	28	29				

NOTES

WATERLOO BRIDGE, GRAY DAY, *1903*

Oil on canvas, 65.1 x 100 cm
Chester Dale Collection
1963.10.183

FEBRUARY

7
MONDAY

8
TUESDAY

9
WEDNESDAY

10
THURSDAY

11
FRIDAY

LINCOLN'S BIRTHDAY

12
SATURDAY

FIRST QUARTER MOON

13
SUNDAY

FEBRUARY	S	M	T	W	T	F	S
			1	2	3	4	5
	6	7	8	9	10	11	12
	13	14	15	16	17	18	19
	20	21	22	23	24	25	26
	27	28	29				

NOTES

FEBRUARY

45

VALENTINE'S DAY

14
MONDAY

46

15
TUESDAY

47

16
WEDNESDAY

48

17
THURSDAY

49

18
FRIDAY

50

19
SATURDAY

FULL MOON

51

20
SUNDAY

NOTES

FEBRUARY

52

PRESIDENTS' DAY

21
MONDAY

53

WASHINGTON'S BIRTHDAY

22
TUESDAY

54

23
WEDNESDAY

55

24
THURSDAY

56

25
FRIDAY

57

26
SATURDAY

58

27
SUNDAY

LAST QUARTER MOON

FEBRUARY	S	M	T	W	T	F	S
			1	2	3	4	5
	6	7	8	9	10	11	12
	13	14	15	16	17	18	19
	20	21	22	23	24	25	26
	27	28	29				

NOTES

THE SEINE AT GIVERNY, *1897*

Oil on canvas, 81.5 x 100.5 cm
Chester Dale Collection
1963.10.180

59

28
MONDAY

60

29
TUESDAY

61

1
WEDNESDAY

62

2
THURSDAY

63

3
FRIDAY

64

4
SATURDAY

65

5
SUNDAY

MARCH

S	M	T	W	T	F	S
			1	2	3	4
5	6	7	8	9	10	11
12	13	14	15	16	17	18
19	20	21	22	23	24	25
26	27	28	29	30	31	

NOTES

MARCH

66
6
MONDAY   NEW MOON

67
7
TUESDAY

68   ASH WEDNESDAY
8
WEDNESDAY

69
9
THURSDAY

70
10
FRIDAY

71
11
SATURDAY

72
12
SUNDAY

NOTES

MARCH

73

13

FIRST QUARTER MOON

74

14
TUESDAY

75

15
WEDNESDAY

76

16
THURSDAY

St. Patrick's Day
Bank Holiday (N. Ireland)

77

17
FRIDAY

78

18
SATURDAY

79

19
SUNDAY

MARCH	S	M	T	W	T	F	S
				1	2	3	4
	5	6	7	8	9	10	11
	12	13	14	15	16	17	18
	19	20	21	22	23	24	25
	26	27	28	29	30	31	

NOTES

The Houses of Parliament, Sunset, *1903*

Oil on canvas, 81.3 x 92.5 cm
Chester Dale Collection
1963.10.48

MARCH

20

FULL MOON
VERNAL EQUINOX 7:35 A.M. (GMT)

MONDAY

21

TUESDAY

22

WEDNESDAY

23

THURSDAY

24

FRIDAY

25

SATURDAY

26

SUNDAY

MARCH

S	M	T	W	T	F	S
			1	2	3	4
5	6	7	8	9	10	11
12	13	14	15	16	17	18
19	20	21	22	23	24	25
26	27	28	29	30	31	

NOTES

WOMAN SEATED UNDER THE WILLOWS, *1880*

Oil on canvas, 81.1 x 60 cm
Chester Dale Collection
1963.10.178

87

27

MONDAY

88

28

LAST QUARTER MOON

TUESDAY

89

29

WEDNESDAY

90

30

THURSDAY

91

31

FRIDAY

92

1

SATURDAY

93

2

DAYLIGHT SAVING TIME BEGINS

SUNDAY

APRIL

S	M	T	W	T	F	S
						1
2	3	4	5	6	7	8
9	10	11	12	13	14	15
16	17	18	19	20	21	22
23 30	24	25	26	27	28	29

NOTES

APRIL

94

3
MONDAY

95

4
TUESDAY   NEW MOON

96

5
WEDNESDAY

97

6
THURSDAY

98

7
FRIDAY

99

8
SATURDAY

100

9
SUNDAY

NOTES

APRIL

10

MONDAY

11

FIRST QUARTER MOON

TUESDAY

12

WEDNESDAY

13

THURSDAY

14

FRIDAY

15

SATURDAY

PALM SUNDAY

16

SUNDAY

APRIL

S	M	T	W	T	F	S
						1
2	3	4	5	6	7	8
9	10	11	12	13	14	15
16	17	18	19	20	21	22
23	24	25	26	27	28	29
30						

NOTES

ROUEN CATHEDRAL, WEST FAÇADE, SUNLIGHT, *1894*

Oil on canvas, 100.1 x 65.8 cm
Chester Dale Collection
1963.10.179

APRIL

17
MONDAY

18
TUESDAY

FULL MOON

PASSOVER (BEGINS AT SUNSET)

19
WEDNESDAY

20
THURSDAY

GOOD FRIDAY

21
FRIDAY

EARTH DAY

22
SATURDAY

EASTER SUNDAY

23
SUNDAY

APRIL	S	M	T	W	T	F	S
							1
	2	3	4	5	6	7	8
	9	10	11	12	13	14	15
	16	17	18	19	20	21	22
	23 30	24	25	26	27	28	29

NOTES

APRIL

24

MONDAY

25

TUESDAY

26

WEDNESDAY

LAST QUARTER MOON

27

THURSDAY

28

FRIDAY

29

SATURDAY

30

SUNDAY

NOTES

MAY

BANK HOLIDAY (UK) 122

1
MONDAY

123

2
TUESDAY

124

3
WEDNESDAY

125

4
THURSDAY

NEW MOON

CINCO DE MAYO 126

5
FRIDAY

127

6
SATURDAY

128

7
SUNDAY

MAY	S	M	T	W	T	F	S
			1	2	3	4	5	6
	7	8	9	10	11	12	13
	14	15	16	17	18	19	20
	21	22	23	24	25	26	27
	28	29	30	31			

NOTES

WOMAN WITH A PARASOL—MADAME MONET AND HER SON, *1875*

Oil on canvas, 100 x 81 cm
Collection of Mr. and Mrs. Paul Mellon
1983.1.29

MAY

8

MONDAY

9

TUESDAY

10

FIRST QUARTER MOON

WEDNESDAY

11

THURSDAY

12

FRIDAY

13

SATURDAY

MOTHER'S DAY

14

SUNDAY

MAY	S	M	T	W	T	F	S
		1	2	3	4	5	6
	7	8	9	10	11	12	13
	14	15	16	17	18	19	20
	21	22	23	24	25	26	27
	28	29	30	31			

NOTES

MAY

136

15
MONDAY

137

16
TUESDAY

138

17
WEDNESDAY

139

18
THURSDAY   FULL MOON

140

19
FRIDAY

141   ARMED FORCES DAY

20
SATURDAY

142

21
SUNDAY

NOTES

Victoria Day (Canada)   *143*

22

MONDAY

144

23

TUESDAY

145

24

WEDNESDAY

146

25

THURSDAY

147

26

LAST QUARTER MOON   FRIDAY

148

27

SATURDAY

149

28

SUNDAY

MAY

S	M	T	W	T	F	S
	1	2	3	4	5	6
7	8	9	10	11	12	13
14	15	16	17	18	19	20
21	22	23	24	25	26	27
28	29	30	31			

NOTES

ARGENTEUIL, *c. 1872*

Oil on canvas, 50.4 x 65.2 cm
Ailsa Mellon Bruce Collection
1970.17.42

MEMORIAL DAY OBSERVED
LATE BANK HOLIDAY (UK)

150

29

MONDAY

MEMORIAL DAY

151

30

TUESDAY

152

31

WEDNESDAY

153

1

THURSDAY

154

2

NEW MOON

FRIDAY

155

3

SATURDAY

156

4

SUNDAY

JUNE

S	M	T	W	T	F	S
				1	2	3
4	5	6	7	8	9	10
11	12	13	14	15	16	17
18	19	20	21	22	23	24
25	26	27	28	29	30	

NOTES

JUNE

157

5
MONDAY

158

6
TUESDAY

159

7
WEDNESDAY

160

8
THURSDAY

161

9
FRIDAY   FIRST QUARTER MOON

162

10
SATURDAY

163

11
SUNDAY

NOTES

JUNE

12

MONDAY

13

TUESDAY

FLAG DAY

14

WEDNESDAY

15

THURSDAY

16

FULL MOON

FRIDAY

17

SATURDAY

FATHER'S DAY

18

SUNDAY

JUNE	S	M	T	W	T	F	S
					1	2	3
	4	5	6	7	8	9	10
	11	12	13	14	15	16	17
	18	19	20	21	22	23	24
	25	26	27	28	29	30	

NOTES

BANKS OF THE SEINE, VÉTHEUIL, *1880*

Oil on canvas, 73.4 x 100.5 cm
Chester Dale Collection
1963.10.177

JUNE

19
MONDAY

20
TUESDAY

21
WEDNESDAY

SUMMER SOLSTICE 1:48 P.M. (GMT)

22
THURSDAY

23
FRIDAY

24
SATURDAY

25
SUNDAY

LAST QUARTER MOON

JUNE

S	M	T	W	T	F	S
				1	2	3
4	5	6	7	8	9	10
11	12	13	14	15	16	17
18	19	20	21	22	23	24
25	26	27	28	29	30	

NOTES

BAZILLE AND CAMILLE (STUDY FOR "DÉJEUNER SUR L'HERBE"), 1865

Oil on canvas, 93 x 68.9 cm
Ailsa Mellon Bruce Collection
1970.17.41

178

26

MONDAY

179

27

TUESDAY

180

28

WEDNESDAY

181

29

THURSDAY

182

30

FRIDAY

Canada Day (Canada)

183

1

NEW MOON

SATURDAY

184

2

SUNDAY

JULY

S	M	T	W	T	F	S
						1
2	3	4	5	6	7	8
9	10	11	12	13	14	15
16	17	18	19	20	21	22
23	24	25	26	27	28	29
30	31					

NOTES

JULY

185   CANADA DAY OBSERVED (CANADA)

3

MONDAY

186   INDEPENDENCE DAY

4

TUESDAY

187

5

WEDNESDAY

188

6

THURSDAY

189

7

FRIDAY

190

8

SATURDAY   FIRST QUARTER MOON

191

9

SUNDAY

NOTES

JULY

192

10

193

11

Bank Holiday (N. Ireland)

194

12

195

13

196

14

197

15

198

16

FULL MOON

JULY

S	M	T	W	T	F	S
						1
2	3	4	5	6	7	8
9	10	11	12	13	14	15
16	17	18	19	20	21	22
23	24	25	26	27	28	29
30	31					

NOTES

THE BRIDGE AT ARGENTEUIL, *1874*

Oil on canvas, 60 x 79.7 cm
Collection of Mr. and Mrs. Paul Mellon
1983.1.24

JULY

199

17
MONDAY

200

18
TUESDAY

201

19
WEDNESDAY

202

20
THURSDAY

203

21
FRIDAY

204

22
SATURDAY

205

23
SUNDAY

JULY

S	M	T	W	T	F	S
						1
2	3	4	5	6	7	8
9	10	11	12	13	14	15
16	17	18	19	20	21	22
23	24	25	26	27	28	29
30	31					

NOTES

JULY

206
24
MONDAY   LAST QUARTER MOON

207
25
TUESDAY

208
26
WEDNESDAY

209
27
THURSDAY

210
28
FRIDAY

211
29
SATURDAY

212
30
SUNDAY

NOTES

213

31

NEW MOON

MONDAY

214

1

TUESDAY

215

2

WEDNESDAY

216

3

THURSDAY

217

4

FRIDAY

218

5

SATURDAY

219

6

SUNDAY

AUGUST

S	M	T	W	T	F	S
		1	2	3	4	5
6	7	8	9	10	11	12
13	14	15	16	17	18	19
20	21	22	23	24	25	26
27	28	29	30	31		

NOTES

The Artist's Garden at Vétheuil, *1880*

Oil on canvas, 151.5 x 121 cm
Ailsa Mellon Bruce Collection
1970.17.45

AUGUST

BANK HOLIDAY (SCOTLAND)

220

7

FIRST QUARTER MOON

MONDAY

221

8

TUESDAY

222

9

WEDNESDAY

223

10

THURSDAY

224

11

FRIDAY

225

12

SATURDAY

226

13

SUNDAY

AUGUST

S	M	T	W	T	F	S
			1	2	3	4	5
6	7	8	9	10	11	12
13	14	15	16	17	18	19
20	21	22	23	24	25	26
27	28	29	30	31		

NOTES

AUGUST

227

14
MONDAY

228

15
TUESDAY   FULL MOON

229

16
WEDNESDAY

230

17
THURSDAY

231

18
FRIDAY

232

19
SATURDAY

233

20
SUNDAY

NOTES

AUGUST

21

MONDAY

22

LAST QUARTER MOON

TUESDAY

23

WEDNESDAY

24

THURSDAY

25

FRIDAY

26

SATURDAY

27

SUNDAY

AUGUST

S	M	T	W	T	F	S
		1	2	3	4	5
6	7	8	9	10	11	12
13	14	15	16	17	18	19
20	21	22	23	24	25	26
27	28	29	30	31		

NOTES

THE ARTIST'S GARDEN IN ARGENTEUIL (A CORNER OF THE GARDEN WITH DAHLIAS), *1873*

Oil on canvas, 61 x 82.5 cm
Gift (Partial and Promised) of Janice H. Levin, in Honor of the 50th Anniversary of the National Gallery of Art
1991.27.1

BANK HOLIDAY (UK)   241

28

MONDAY

242

29

TUESDAY

NEW MOON   243

30

WEDNESDAY

244

31

THURSDAY

245

1

FRIDAY

246

2

SATURDAY

247

3

SUNDAY

SEPTEMBER

S	M	T	W	T	F	S
					1	2
3	4	5	6	7	8	9
10	11	12	13	14	15	16
17	18	19	20	21	22	23
24	25	26	27	28	29	30

NOTES

SEPTEMBER

248

4
MONDAY

249

5
TUESDAY

FIRST QUARTER MOON

250

6
WEDNESDAY

251

7
THURSDAY

252

8
FRIDAY

253

9
SATURDAY

254

10
SUNDAY

NOTES

SEPTEMBER

255

11
MONDAY

256

12
TUESDAY

257

13
WEDNESDAY

FULL MOON

258

14
THURSDAY

259

15
FRIDAY

260

16
SATURDAY

261

17
SUNDAY

SEPTEMBER

S	M	T	W	T	F	S
					1	2
3	4	5	6	7	8	9
10	11	12	13	14	15	16
17	18	19	20	21	22	23
24	25	26	27	28	29	30

NOTES

THE JAPANESE FOOTBRIDGE, *1899*

Oil on canvas, 81.3 x 101.6 cm
Gift of Victoria Nebeker Coberly, in memory of her son John W. Mudd, and Walter H. and Leonore Annenberg
1992.9.1

SEPTEMBER

18

MONDAY

19

TUESDAY

20

WEDNESDAY

21

LAST QUARTER MOON

THURSDAY

22

AUTUMNAL EQUINOX 5:27 P.M. (GMT)

FRIDAY

23

SATURDAY

24

SUNDAY

SEPTEMBER	S	M	T	W	T	F	S
						1	2
	3	4	5	6	7	8	9
	10	11	12	13	14	15	16
	17	18	19	20	21	22	23
	24	25	26	27	28	29	30

NOTES

SHIPS RIDING ON THE SEINE AT ROUEN, *1872/1873*

Oil on canvas, 37.8 x 46.6 cm
Ailsa Mellon Bruce Collection
1970.17.43

269

25
MONDAY

270

26
TUESDAY

271

27
NEW MOON   WEDNESDAY

272

28
THURSDAY

273
ROSH HASHANAH (BEGINS AT SUNSET)

29
FRIDAY

274

30
SATURDAY

275

1
SUNDAY

OCTOBER

S	M	T	W	T	F	S
1	2	3	4	5	6	7
8	9	10	11	12	13	14
15	16	17	18	19	20	21
22	23	24	25	26	27	28
29	30	31				

NOTES

OCTOBER

276

2
MONDAY

277

3
TUESDAY

278

4
WEDNESDAY

279

5
THURSDAY   FIRST QUARTER MOON

280

6
FRIDAY

281

7
SATURDAY

282   YOM KIPPUR (BEGINS AT SUNSET)

8
SUNDAY

NOTES

OCTOBER

COLUMBUS DAY OBSERVED
THANKSGIVING DAY (CANADA)

9

MONDAY

10

TUESDAY

11

WEDNESDAY

COLUMBUS DAY

12

THURSDAY

13

FULL MOON

FRIDAY

14

SATURDAY

15

SUNDAY

OCTOBER

S	M	T	W	T	F	S
1	2	3	4	5	6	7
8	9	10	11	12	13	14
15	16	17	18	19	20	21
22	23	24	25	26	27	28
29	30	31				

NOTES

PALAZZO DA MULA, VENICE, *1908*

Oil on canvas, 62 x 81.1 cm
Chester Dale Collection
1963.10.182

OCTOBER

16

MONDAY

17

TUESDAY

18

WEDNESDAY

19

THURSDAY

20

LAST QUARTER MOON

FRIDAY

21

SATURDAY

22

SUNDAY

OCTOBER	S	M	T	W	T	F	S
		1	2	3	4	5	6	7
	8	9	10	11	12	13	14
	15	16	17	18	19	20	21
	22	23	24	25	26	27	28
	29	30	31				

NOTES

OCTOBER

23
MONDAY

24
TUESDAY   UNITED NATIONS DAY

25
WEDNESDAY

26
THURSDAY

27
FRIDAY   NEW MOON

28
SATURDAY

29
SUNDAY   DAYLIGHT SAVING TIME ENDS

NOTES

304

30

MONDAY

HALLOWEEN

305

31

TUESDAY

306

1

WEDNESDAY

307

2

THURSDAY

308

3

FRIDAY

309

4

FIRST QUARTER MOON

SATURDAY

310

5

SUNDAY

NOVEMBER	S	M	T	W	T	F	S
				1	2	3	4
	5	6	7	8	9	10	11
	12	13	14	15	16	17	18
	19	20	21	22	23	24	25
	26	27	28	29	30		

NOTES

Jerusalem Artichoke Flowers, *1880*

Oil on canvas, 99.6 x 73 cm
Chester Dale Collection
1963.10.181

NOVEMBER

6

MONDAY

Election Day

7

TUESDAY

8

WEDNESDAY

9

THURSDAY

Veterans Day Observed

10

FRIDAY

Veterans Day
Remembrance Day (Canada)

11

SATURDAY

Full Moon

12

SUNDAY

NOVEMBER	S	M	T	W	T	F	S
				1	2	3	4
	5	6	7	8	9	10	11
	12	13	14	15	16	17	18
	19	20	21	22	23	24	25
	26	27	28	29	30		

NOTES

NOVEMBER

318   REMEMBRANCE DAY OBSERVED (CANADA)

13
MONDAY

319

14
TUESDAY

320

15
WEDNESDAY

321

16
THURSDAY

322

17
FRIDAY

323

18
SATURDAY   LAST QUARTER MOON

324

19
SUNDAY

NOTES

325

20

MONDAY

326

21

TUESDAY

327

22

WEDNESDAY

Thanksgiving Day

328

23

THURSDAY

329

24

FRIDAY

330

25

New Moon

SATURDAY

331

26

SUNDAY

NOVEMBER	S	M	T	W	T	F	S
				1	2	3	4
	5	6	7	8	9	10	11
	12	13	14	15	16	17	18
	19	20	21	22	23	24	25
	26	27	28	29	30		

NOTES

Interior, after Dinner, *1868/1869*

Oil on canvas, 50.5 x 65.7 cm
Collection of Mr. and Mrs. Paul Mellon
1983.1.26

332

27
MONDAY

333

28
TUESDAY

334

29
WEDNESDAY

335

30
THURSDAY

336

1
FRIDAY

337

2
SATURDAY

338

3
SUNDAY

DECEMBER	S	M	T	W	T	F	S
						1	2
	3	4	5	6	7	8	9
	10	11	12	13	14	15	16
	17	18	19	20	21	22	23
	24	25	26	27	28	29	30
	31						

NOTES

DECEMBER

339

4
MONDAY   FIRST QUARTER MOON

340

5
TUESDAY

341

6
WEDNESDAY

342

7
THURSDAY

343

8
FRIDAY

344

9
SATURDAY

345

10
SUNDAY

NOTES

DECEMBER

11

FULL MOON

12

13

14

15

16

17

DECEMBER

S	M	T	W	T	F	S
					1	2
3	4	5	6	7	8	9
10	11	12	13	14	15	16
17	18	19	20	21	22	23
24	25	26	27	28	29	30
31						

NOTES

ROUEN CATHEDRAL, WEST FAÇADE, *1894*

Oil on canvas, 100.1 x 65.9 cm
Chester Dale Collection
1963.10.49

DECEMBER

353

18

LAST QUARTER MOON

MONDAY

354

19

TUESDAY

355

20

WEDNESDAY

HANUKKAH (BEGINS AT SUNSET)

356

21

WINTER SOLSTICE 1:37 P.M. (GMT)

THURSDAY

357

22

FRIDAY

358

23

SATURDAY

359

24

SUNDAY

DECEMBER

S	M	T	W	T	F	S
					1	2
3	4	5	6	7	8	9
10	11	12	13	14	15	16
17	18	19	20	21	22	23
24	25	26	27	28	29	30
31						

NOTES

DECEMBER

360   CHRISTMAS DAY

25
MONDAY   NEW MOON

361   KWANZAA BEGINS
BOXING DAY (CANADA, UK)

26
TUESDAY

362

27
WEDNESDAY

363

28
THURSDAY

364

29
FRIDAY

365

30
SATURDAY

366

31
SUNDAY

NOTES

2000

JANUARY

S	M	T	W	T	F	S
						1
2	3	4	5	6	7	8
9	10	11	12	13	14	15
16	17	18	19	20	21	22
23	24	25	26	27	28	29
30	31					

MAY

S	M	T	W	T	F	S
	1	2	3	4	5	6
7	8	9	10	11	12	13
14	15	16	17	18	19	20
21	22	23	24	25	26	27
28	29	30	31			

SEPTEMBER

S	M	T	W	T	F	S
					1	2
3	4	5	6	7	8	9
10	11	12	13	14	15	16
17	18	19	20	21	22	23
24	25	26	27	28	29	30

FEBRUARY

S	M	T	W	T	F	S
		1	2	3	4	5
6	7	8	9	10	11	12
13	14	15	16	17	18	19
20	21	22	23	24	25	26
27	28	29				

JUNE

S	M	T	W	T	F	S
				1	2	3
4	5	6	7	8	9	10
11	12	13	14	15	16	17
18	19	20	21	22	23	24
25	26	27	28	29	30	

OCTOBER

S	M	T	W	T	F	S
1	2	3	4	5	6	7
8	9	10	11	12	13	14
15	16	17	18	19	20	21
22	23	24	25	26	27	28
29	30	31				

MARCH

S	M	T	W	T	F	S
			1	2	3	4
5	6	7	8	9	10	11
12	13	14	15	16	17	18
19	20	21	22	23	24	25
26	27	28	29	30	31	

JULY

S	M	T	W	T	F	S
						1
2	3	4	5	6	7	8
9	10	11	12	13	14	15
16	17	18	19	20	21	22
23	24	25	26	27	28	29
30	31					

NOVEMBER

S	M	T	W	T	F	S
			1	2	3	4
5	6	7	8	9	10	11
12	13	14	15	16	17	18
19	20	21	22	23	24	25
26	27	28	29	30		

APRIL

S	M	T	W	T	F	S
						1
2	3	4	5	6	7	8
9	10	11	12	13	14	15
16	17	18	19	20	21	22
23	24	25	26	27	28	29
30						

AUGUST

S	M	T	W	T	F	S
		1	2	3	4	5
6	7	8	9	10	11	12
13	14	15	16	17	18	19
20	21	22	23	24	25	26
27	28	29	30	31		

DECEMBER

S	M	T	W	T	F	S
					1	2
3	4	5	6	7	8	9
10	11	12	13	14	15	16
17	18	19	20	21	22	23
24	25	26	27	28	29	30
31						

2001

JANUARY

S	M	T	W	T	F	S
	1	2	3	4	5	6
7	8	9	10	11	12	13
14	15	16	17	18	19	20
21	22	23	24	25	26	27
28	29	30	31			

FEBRUARY

S	M	T	W	T	F	S
				1	2	3
4	5	6	7	8	9	10
11	12	13	14	15	16	17
18	19	20	21	22	23	24
25	26	27	28			

MARCH

S	M	T	W	T	F	S
				1	2	3
4	5	6	7	8	9	10
11	12	13	14	15	16	17
18	19	20	21	22	23	24
25	26	27	28	29	30	31

APRIL

S	M	T	W	T	F	S
1	2	3	4	5	6	7
8	9	10	11	12	13	14
15	16	17	18	19	20	21
22	23	24	25	26	27	28
29	30					

MAY

S	M	T	W	T	F	S
		1	2	3	4	5
6	7	8	9	10	11	12
13	14	15	16	17	18	19
20	21	22	23	24	25	26
27	28	29	30	31		

JUNE

S	M	T	W	T	F	S
					1	2
3	4	5	6	7	8	9
10	11	12	13	14	15	16
17	18	19	20	21	22	23
24	25	26	27	28	29	30

JULY

S	M	T	W	T	F	S
1	2	3	4	5	6	7
8	9	10	11	12	13	14
15	16	17	18	19	20	21
22	23	24	25	26	27	28
29	30	31				

AUGUST

S	M	T	W	T	F	S
			1	2	3	4
5	6	7	8	9	10	11
12	13	14	15	16	17	18
19	20	21	22	23	24	25
26	27	28	29	30	31	

SEPTEMBER

S	M	T	W	T	F	S
						1
2	3	4	5	6	7	8
9	10	11	12	13	14	15
16	17	18	19	20	21	22
23	24	25	26	27	28	29
30						

OCTOBER

S	M	T	W	T	F	S
	1	2	3	4	5	6
7	8	9	10	11	12	13
14	15	16	17	18	19	20
21	22	23	24	25	26	27
28	29	30	31			

NOVEMBER

S	M	T	W	T	F	S
				1	2	3
4	5	6	7	8	9	10
11	12	13	14	15	16	17
18	19	20	21	22	23	24
25	26	27	28	29	30	

DECEMBER

S	M	T	W	T	F	S
						1
2	3	4	5	6	7	8
9	10	11	12	13	14	15
16	17	18	19	20	21	22
23	24	25	26	27	28	29
30	31					

PERSONAL INFORMATION

Name _____

Address _____

City _____

State _____

Zip _____

Phone _____

Fax _____

Email _____

In case of emergency, please notify:

Name _____

Address _____

City _____

State _____

Zip _____

Phone _____

Medical information:

Physician's name _____

Physician's phone _____

Health insurance company _____

Plan number _____

Allergies _____

Other _____

Other information:

Driver's license number _____

Car insurance company _____

Policy number _____